Paul
the man and the mission

NICK FAWCETT

**kevin
mayhew**

First published in 2002 by
KEVIN MAYHEW LTD
Buxhall, Stowmarket, Suffolk IP14 3BW
Email: info@kevinmayhewltd.com

9 8 7 6 5 4 3 2 1 0

ISBN 1 84003 916 7
Catalogue No 1500508

Cover design by Angela Selfe
Edited by Katherine Laidler
Typesetting by Louise Selfe

Printed and bound in Great Britain

Contents

To Dave Bell
with thanks for your invaluable contribution
to so many study sessions during my time at Gas Green
and for all your help in numerous other ways.

Acknowledgements

The publishers wish to express their thanks to Cambridge University Press, The Edinburgh Building, Shaftesbury Road, Cambridge, CB2 2RU, for permission to reproduce the extract from The Book of Common Prayer (adapted), the rights in which are vested in the Crown.

Bible quotations are taken from the New Revised Standard Version of the Bible, copyright © 1989 by the Division of Christian Education of the National Council of the Churches of Christ in the USA. Used by permission. All rights reserved.

Introduction

If you had been a Christian in the earliest days of the Church, who, I wonder, would you have considered the most likely person to carry the faith forward. Perhaps you'd have chosen Peter, the one Jesus had called 'the rock of the Church'; dynamic, impulsive, clearly filled with the power of the Holy Spirit. Perhaps you'd have favoured John, beloved disciple of Jesus and ready to stick his neck out for the sake of the gospel. Or maybe Matthew, the man whose life probably more than any other of the twelve had been turned upside down by Jesus. Perhaps, instead, you'd have gone for one of the seven chosen to oversee administration within the Church: one such as Philip, whose powerful preaching was so clearly able to touch people's lives, or Stephen, who, before his death, promised to make a similar impact.

The one person you wouldn't have suggested is Paul, or Saul as he was otherwise known. That name would have struck fear into your heart, for he was the avowed enemy of the Christian faith, resolved to wipe out the Church through every means at his disposal. The news of his part in the stoning of Stephen would almost certainly have reached your ears, so when he set off for Damascus, 'still breathing threats and murder against the disciples of the Lord' (Acts 9:1), you would have feared the worst, convinced there was to be yet more pain and suffering. If God was unable to use anyone, it was surely Saul. If anyone was irredeemable, a lost cause, again it had to be Saul. Yet this, of course, is the man who arguably contributed more to the growth of the Church than anyone else in history; whose writings make up nearly half of the New Testament; who carried the gospel across much of the Roman empire; and who almost certainly ended up sacrificing his life for his faith. It is the sort of story that, were we to read it in the pages of a child's comic or Mills and Boon romance, would bring a smile to our faces. A lovely idea, a wonderful twist in the tale, but strictly in the realm of fantasy; the sort of thing that may happen in the world of the imagination but not in the real world. Yet, undeniably, indisputably, it happened. Paul was to become a committed follower of Christ in one of the most dramatic and total transformations in history; his life turned inside out and upside down.

To do justice to his life and mission in six studies is frankly impossible, for there is so much we could say about Paul: so many aspects to his character and so much he has contributed to our understanding of faith. Instead, I have chosen six themes that reflect aspects of the man and his mission. We look first at the story of his conversion and draw from this an important precondition of Christian discipleship: a willingness to admit our need of Christ and turn away from our former way of life. Next, we turn to Paul's outpouring of frustration in Romans 7 concerning his inability to be the person he longed to be; an outpouring that gives way to the final triumphant recognition that forgiveness depends on grace rather than works. We move to Paul's likening of the Christian life to the training regime of an athlete, and then, in the fourth session, we focus on perhaps the best known of all Paul's writings, the celebrated passage on love from 1 Corinthians 13. Session five explores the theme of contentment, and then finally we look at one of the more unusual incidents of Paul's ministry – a somewhat unsuccessful 'preaching engagement' in Troas that reminds us nonetheless of the ingredient that, perhaps more than any other, contributed to his legacy: namely, an overwhelming desire to share his faith.

For many, the Apostle Paul can seem a somewhat daunting figure, his theology complex and his teaching difficult to understand. It is my hope that this book will bring out the other side to Paul: the ordinary person like you or me whose faith, vision and devotion still has so much to teach us in our continuing journey of discipleship.

Nick Fawcett

Leader's notes

I suggest using the material in this book as follows:

- Each session begins with a traditional prayer, followed by a short paragraph introducing the overall theme. It is worth reading this aloud, to set the scene for the session.

- After this I have included 'Activity' sessions, designed to break the ice and to encourage informal reflection on the theme of the study. Allow ten minutes or so for these, but do not allow them to dominate the session.

- Next comes a Bible passage (my own paraphrase unless otherwise stated). This should be read aloud, and then time given for group members to quietly ponder its meaning.

- Ideally, group members need to have read the 'Comment' section before the meeting, in which case you will need to have circulated booklets in advance of the first session. Alternatively, extend the period of quiet after the reading so that participants can read this section at their own pace.

- The 'Summary' section highlights the key points of the Comment. The leader should read this aloud before inviting people's thoughts on the subject so far.

- Allow discussion to develop, and introduce as appropriate the questions provided in the Discussion section. It may be appropriate at this point to bring in the passage suggested for further reading, though you may prefer to leave this, as I have done, to round off the theme nearer the end.

- Pause for prayer, using the prayer provided, a prayer of your own, or a time of quiet/open prayer.

- After allowing ample time for discussion, read the meditation to draw people's thoughts together. The meditation in week 6 was written specially for this book; the others are taken from my earlier publications *No Ordinary Man* (books 1 and 2).

- Briefly outline the suggestions for action. Invite any further ideas from among the group. From the second week onwards, you might also give people the opportunity to share how they applied the suggestions from the previous week.
- Finally, end the meeting in prayer, using either the prayer provided or your own.

Prayer

Loving God,
    we thank you for the Apostle Paul
    and all that you teach us through his example.
We thank you for the way you turned his life around,
    using him in ways far beyond his expectations,
    proclaiming the gospel through his life and ministry,
    speaking to innumerable people in his own time
    and to countless generations since.
We thank you that his words still have power
    to move and challenge, even today,
    challenging, nurturing, teaching and guiding us
    in our own journeys of discipleship.
We may not have his gifts, faith, energy or vision,
    but you call us as you called him,
    and you can use us too in ways beyond our imagining.
Help us, then, to learn from his experiences,
    to hear your voice through his testimony,
    and to respond to your love,
    to the glory of your name.
Amen.

First week

Admitting we're wrong

Prayer

O Lord and master of my life,
  give me grace to see my own errors and not to judge others,
  for you are blessed from all ages to all ages.
Amen.

Excerpt from Eastern Orthodox prayer

Introduction

When did you last get something hopelessly wrong? I don't just mean some careless mistake – a mishap here, an error there – but when did you last make a complete fool of yourself? Perhaps you were involved in an argument in which you vehemently insisted you were right, only to realise you were wrong. Perhaps you have trumpeted passionately held convictions, only to realise that they were misplaced. Perhaps you have caused hurt to someone, which, given more thought, you could have avoided. Whatever it may have been, I expect we all have moments the memory of which makes us want to curl up in embarrassment. Let me move on, though, to another and more important question. When did you last _admit_ to someone that you've been wrong? If you're anything like me, such moments are harder to recall, for though it is relatively easy to acknowledge mistakes to ourselves, it is much harder admitting them to others. Yet that is what we see in the story of the Apostle Paul: someone who faced up to the truth about himself. A point came in his life when he had to accept that he had been horribly and hideously wrong, that he had made a most appalling mistake and needed to start again. Thankfully, he had the courage to do just that, and his example provides an ongoing challenge to us all.

Activity

Slippery spellings (see page 67).

Reading: Galatians 1:13-17, 22-24

You know all about my conduct when in Judaism – how I single-mindedly persecuted and tried to destroy the Church of God, and how I progressed in Judaism beyond many of my fellow-Jews, being fanatical in the defence of the traditions of our ancestors. When, though, the one who elected me from my mother's womb chose by his grace to reveal his Son through me, so that I might preach him among the nations, I did not discuss it with anyone, or go to Jerusalem to meet with those who were Apostles before me, but went away to Arabia before returning to Damascus. I was unknown then except by name to the churches of Judea, they having heard only that the former persecutor was now preaching the very faith he had attacked, and they praised God because of me.

Comment

The newsreader could hardly keep back a smile. Incredibly, a team of scientists studying BSE had spent four years studying the brains of cows thinking that they came from sheep. It was a monumental blunder and one the government would no doubt have dearly liked to keep quiet, but it had no choice other than to go public, for had it attempted to conceal the facts, only for the truth later to come out, the outcry would have been immeasurable. Most of us can evade unpleasant truths more easily. Instead of acknowledging a mistake, we push it under the carpet. Instead of saying sorry, we keep our heads down and wait for the storm to blow over. Instead of facing up to an awkward challenge, we prefer instead to live a lie. Why? Because, on the surface at least, it is easier that way, avoiding embarrassment and humiliation, not to mention the need to change. Although it may seem easier, however, such a response condemns us to a lifetime weighed down by guilt and unease; a life in which true peace and fulfilment constantly elude us. The Apostle Paul affords us a glimpse of an alternative and infinitely more rewarding response, if only we have the courage to make it.

Schooled as a Pharisee from his earliest days, trained by one of the leading rabbis of his time, and groomed for great things within his faith, Paul (or Saul as he was then more commonly known) had made the destruction of the infant Christian Church his over-riding mission in life. In his eyes, the message of the gospel was a shocking blasphemy and a direct threat to his heritage – one he was determined to resist at all costs – and so, with a burning desire to destroy Christians wherever he found them, he set off towards Damascus. Only, suddenly, the ground was pulled from under his feet, as midway through his journey he was confronted by Jesus in those simple words: 'Saul, Saul, why do you persecute me?' At that moment, the awful truth must have dawned: he had been wrong. In one unexpected encounter, everything he had believed and worked for was thrust into the melting pot, for to acknowledge that Jesus was calling him meant accepting he had made a mistake. Would he have the courage to admit it? The answer was yes. What of us: are we ready to answer likewise; to see ourselves as we really are, without excuses or pretence, and to admit where we too have been wrong?

If Paul, though, had to face up personally to his mistakes, he also had to acknowledge them before God, and, in some ways, that must have been harder still. We may not immediately think so, for surely Paul regularly made time for confession, just as we do, none of us under any illusions that everything in our lives is as it should be. Paul was no different, as we shall see in our next session. He was well aware that he fell short of what God requires – perhaps more aware than most of us – so why should he struggle to admit this most fundamental mistake of all? The answer comes down to honesty. There are some things we are happy to confess, and others we would rather not face up to. There are sins we try to do something about, and others we pretend aren't even there. To be honest before God, truly open before him, risks having our life turned upside down and inside out, for we cannot confess our faults and then do nothing about them. So it was for Paul. He had to accept that instead of serving God throughout his life, he had been fighting against him. He had to hear what God was saying and come to terms with the fact that it pointed him in an entirely new direction. Would he have the courage to do that? The answer is yes, and, once more, his response asks us: are we prepared to do the same?

Admitting his mistakes, to himself and to God, was costly and demanding, yet the hardest part was yet to come, for what Paul finally had to do was admit to others he had been wrong, and we can scarcely imagine how difficult that must have been. Put yourself into his shoes: Paul, the archetypal Pharisee and destroyer of the Church *par excellence*, having publicly to declare his newfound faith in Christ. It must have been hard enough contemplating the inevitable reaction of friends and colleagues back at home, picturing them throwing up their hands or shaking their heads in disbelief. To stand before them and declare that had he been wrong, that he was a different person from the one they thought they knew, must have taken some doing. It must have been harder still facing those who had lived in fear of him and whose loved ones had very possibly suffered at his hands. This was the acid test, the proof of his sincerity: whether he would be willing to eat humble pie, go to those he'd cursed, condemned and persecuted, and say to them, 'Forgive me, I've been wrong.' Would he have the courage to face that challenge? The answer is yes, and again it asks us if we have the courage to do likewise.

If we want to be the people God would have us be, we must be ready to admit our mistakes not just to ourselves or to God but to those we have wronged. We will not find that easy – quite the contrary. It is far easier to brazen it out, cover things up or pretend they never happened. Yet if we, like Paul, are serious about responding to Christ, and about being at one with ourselves, with God and with one another, then there are times when we must be ready to say, humbly and sincerely, 'I've been wrong.' In Paul, we see a willingness to do just that. Are we ready to follow his lead?

Summary

- Admitting our mistakes isn't easy, yet ultimately concealing them is harder still.
- To put our mistakes behind us involves admitting them first to ourselves.
- We need also to admit our mistakes to God, even though doing so may prove demanding, leading to a complete change in our lives.
- There are times when we need to admit our mistakes to those we have wronged, if we are to put them behind us.
- Have we the courage to admit we're wrong?

Discussion

- Are there mistakes we have made that continue to haunt us? Do we have the moral fibre needed to admit these, even when it involves embarrassment and humiliation?
- Which do we find hardest: acknowledging our mistakes before God, to ourselves or to others?
- Are you burdened by a sense of guilt over past mistakes? Isn't it time you let go and trusted in God's forgiveness?
- Is it enough simply to confess our sins to God, or does true confession need to involve acknowledging our mistakes and saying sorry to those we have sinned against if it is to be anything more than pious platitudes?
- Are there ever times when we ought to keep quiet about our faults, if revealing them would cause unnecessary distress to others?

Prayer

Sovereign God,
    we find it so hard to acknowledge our mistakes,
    to admit that we are as fallible as the next person.
When we know we have done wrong, we run from the truth,
    unwilling or afraid to face facts.
Afraid of losing face, we go on pretending,
    adding one falsehood to another,
    denying our mistakes or attempting to excuse them.
We concern ourselves with outer appearances
    rather than with inner reality,
    attempting to convince ourselves that all is well,
    even though we know in our hearts that it is not as it should be.
Forgive us our dishonesty and cowardice.
Give us the wisdom and humility we need to recognise our mistakes,
    to acknowledge them openly,
    to seek forgiveness,
    and, where possible, to make amends.
Through Jesus Christ our Lord.
Amen.

Meditation of Paul

I was wrong,
    so terribly, totally wrong,
    and now I'm sick with shame.
To think that I, Paul, persecuted the Messiah;
    the one for whom we had waited so long,
    the one whom we all longed to see.
I failed to recognise him,
    blinded by my own pride and bigotry.
I'd watched as his followers were killed,
    rejoicing in their deaths,
    glad to be associated with their destruction.

16

And then, when the opportunity finally came,
    I leapt at the chance to destroy them myself.
It was my mission,
      my great calling,
      and I pursued it gleefully,
      brutally,
      with unquenchable zeal.
They quaked at the sound of my voice, those Christians,
    and I gave glory to God.
They trembled as I approached,
    and I offered him my gratitude.
I have broken bodies,
      tormented minds,
      crushed spirits,
      all in the name of faith.
But then I saw it,
      there in the brightness,
      the face of Jesus,
      tears in his eyes.
I heard it,
      there in the silence,
      the voice of Jesus:
      'Why, Saul, why?'
And I knew then the awful, wonderful truth.
It was just as they had said:
      he was the Messiah,
      risen from the dead.
I know that now, but I wish I didn't,
    for *I* have become the one suffering,
    racked by guilt and sorrow.
Why did he spare me to endure this agony?
Why not finish me off there and then?
Or is this my punishment,
    his judgement on my foul, despicable crimes?
There's no way he can ever forgive me, I'm certain of that,
    not after all I've done.

And even if he did,
>there's no way I could ever be accepted by his followers;
>they'd never believe someone like me could change that much.
So here I am:
>Paul, persecutor of Christ,
>grovelling in misery before him;
>Paul, exterminator of the Church,
>wishing I could be exterminated.
I was wrong, so terribly wrong,
>but it's too late for excuses,
>too late for tears,
>too late to make amends,
>too late for anything.

Further reading: Psalm 32:1-5

Happy is the one whose wrongdoing is forgiven, whose faults are covered. Happy is the one to whom the Lord ascribes no guilt, and in whose spirit there is no pretence. While I remained silent, my body grew weary with my constant groaning, for day and night your hand weighed heavily upon me; my strength dried up like sap in the heat of summer. Then I acknowledged my sin and did not conceal my guilt from you; I said, 'I will confess my disobedience to the Lord', and you absolved me from my guilt and sin.

Suggestions for action

If you have wronged somebody, apologise. If you have made a mistake, admit it. If you are haunted by a guilty secret, face up to it. If you are conscious that something is coming between you and God, confess it and seek his forgiveness. Stop meaning to do something; act now!

Closing prayer

Sovereign God,
    when we do wrong,
    give us courage to acknowledge it before you and others,
    so that we may know your forgiveness
    and open a way to the healing of the wounds
    our mistakes have caused.
Through Jesus Christ our Lord.
Amen.

Second week

By the grace of God

Opening prayer

Father in heaven,
    hold not our sins up against us
    but hold us up against our sins,
    so that the thought of you when it wakens in our soul,
    and each time it wakens,
    should not remind us of what we have committed
    but of what you have forgiven,
    not of how we went astray
    but of how you have saved us.
Amen.

Søren Kirkegaard

Introduction

Do you remember the television series years ago called *It's a Knock-out*? Fronted by Eddie Waring and Stuart Hall, the programme swiftly became a smash hit, as did its European counterpart, *Jeux sans Frontières*. Teams from across Britain and Europe took part in a variety of games, ranging from picking up an egg with a JCB to pillow fights on a narrow beam, in which the loser was dispatched into a pool of icy water. Perhaps the most common sight, however, and the one that endures most in people's memory, was that of competitors struggling to run up a greased ramp while attached to a strong piece of elastic. Numerous variants of this idea were employed across the years, audiences taking unerring delight in the sight of some hapless individual getting within inches of their goal only to be yanked back at the last moment and to slither wretchedly back down to whence they had started!

There is a sense in which as Christians we can feel ourselves to be in much the same predicament. Our objective is clear enough – to follow Christ faithfully – and we strive to do that to the best of our ability, yet always, it seems, there is something holding us back. Just when we think we are getting close, life brings us down to earth with a bump. Just when we believe we're making progress, the ground slips from beneath us, and we find ourselves sliding away. It's easy at such times to lose heart, convinced that nothing has changed, that we're the same people we always used to be. In a way that's true, for, as the Apostle Paul was well aware, the old self lives on in Christians along with the new. We do not suddenly become better people, everything about us miraculously perfect; still less can we hope to change through our own efforts. Faith ultimately hinges not on what *we* may do but on what Jesus has done. Human effort, however well intended, can never put us right with God; that is down simply to his grace.

Activity

Word puzzle (see page 68).

Reading: Romans 7:15, 19-25

I do not understand why I act as I do. For I end up doing the things I hate rather than the things I want to do . . . I do evil instead of the good I wish to do. If I do what I don't want to do, it is not I personally who do it so much as the sin dwelling within me. I find it to be a law that whenever I intend to do good, evil is there as well, for, while, deep within, I delight in the law of God, I see a different law in my body that battles with the law of my mind, holding me captive to the law of sin that dwells in my members. What a wretched man I am! Who will deliver me from this body of death? Thanks be to God through Jesus Christ our Lord!

Comment

'I'm sorry. I won't do it again.' How often have you said some-thing like that, and how often have the words returned to haunt you? Fine resolutions are easy to make; putting them into practice is an altogether different matter. Whether it be kicking a habit, overcoming a weakness or striving to turn over a new leaf, effecting real and lasting change is much harder than we might at first imagine.

To a point, that's precisely what the Apostle Paul was saying in his letter to the Romans; a fact which, when you stop to think about it, comes as rather a surprise, given the remarkable transformation that had taken place in his life. Remember that this is the man whose life was revolutionised through his encounter with Jesus; the one who, almost overnight, turned from being a persecutor to ambassador of the Church, from avowed enemy to devoted servant of Christ. You simply can't change much more than that! Yet, in his words to the Church in Rome, we find Paul pouring out his heart and soul, to all intents and purposes wringing his hands in abject despair as he looks at his life and grieves over his failings. How can this be? How do we begin to reconcile such starkly contrasting pictures?

The conundrum becomes yet more baffling when we recall that, by his own admission, Paul's conduct in terms of the Jewish law had been exemplary. 'If anyone else has reason to be confident in the flesh,' he says, 'I have more . . . as to righteousness under the law, blameless' (Philippians 3:4b, 6b, *NRSV*). So what's going on here? What was such an apparent paragon of virtue doing bewailing his faults? The answer, of course, lies beneath the surface: in the thoughts of the heart, the self that lies hidden from public view, the attitudes, instincts and innate predispositions that together make us what we are. Paul knew that we can outwardly seem right with God yet inwardly be estranged; that it is possible to do the right things for all the wrong reasons. He had caught a glimpse of the way life could be in Christ, and he was painfully aware how far his life fell short of the mark.

If that was true of Paul, how much more do we know it to be

true of ourselves, for most of us find not just the inward part hard but the outward side too. We mean to stay true, but temptation catches us unawares. We intend to respond, only for our attention to be distracted. We aim to be more loving, more faithful, less weak, less foolish, only to go on making the same mistakes time and time again. There comes a point when we find ourselves, like Paul, crying out in despair and frustration: 'Not again!' It's hard not to lose heart at such times, and harder still not to feel that God will do the same. 'Why has nothing changed?' we ask ourselves. 'How is it that I'm no different than I used to be?' Inevitably, we find ourselves wondering how much longer God can go on showing us forgiveness, or whether the time will come when he says enough is enough and washes his hands of us. Yet it is at just this point that Paul takes us to the heart of the gospel, as he lurches from an outpouring of despair to a sudden and spontaneous surge of praise. 'What a wretched man I am! Who will deliver me from this body of death? Thanks be to God through Jesus Christ our Lord!'

In Christ, he had found acceptance as he was, despite all that was wrong in his life. He wasn't suddenly perfect, immune from temptation, squeaky clean, whiter than white. He was still frail, fallible and human, but, by the grace of God, he had discovered a love that reached out to him as he was and offered the possibility of him becoming the person he longed to become. The old self lived on, but he was nonetheless a new creation, God's Spirit nurturing new life within him. Salvation, he tells us, is not something we earn but that God invites us to receive. It is his gift in Christ: for you, for me, for *everyone*. What *we* can never hope to do, *he* has decisively achieved through his living, dying and rising among us in Christ. No wonder Paul ended his outburst of frustration in that triumphant explosion of thanksgiving!

To explore everything that we could draw from Paul's testimony for us today would take a book far bigger than this one, but there are two points that, for me, stand out, and the first is this: don't be too hard on yourself. Strange though it may seem, we can often be our own hardest critics. Where others are prepared to forgive and forget, we remorselessly castigate ourselves over the smallest fault.

Where others are ready to make allowances, we set impossible standards to live up to, turning discipleship into a heavy load rather than a release from our burdens. How many people, I wonder, fail to commit themselves to Christ or to their local church because they feel that somehow they are not good enough? How many continue to wrestle with a sense of guilt, rather than find liberation in the simple message of the gospel? How many persist in viewing God as a vengeful and forbidding ogre, rather than one who delights in showing mercy and sharing his love? This is not to encourage complacency or to say that we should not strive to change, but we should do that in joyful response, not desperate duty. We yearn faithfully to follow, yet we know we will continue to fall. The wonder is that we know also that God will always be there to pick us up again and lead us on. Faith, finally, is not about what we may do but what he has done!

Secondly, and equally important, don't be too hard on others. A Christian is not, or at least should not be, someone who claims to be better than other people. There should be no sense of superiority, no suggestion of being more worthy or more deserving than anyone else. On the contrary, to declare our faith in Christ and commit our life to him means to recognise our weakness, to accept our fallibility, and to admit our total dependence upon God's grace. Unless faith begins and ends there, then we will have a false picture of what discipleship is all about, and, much worse, give a false picture to others. It is one of the great tragedies of the Church that it has become associated in many people's minds with holier-than-thou, self-righteousness and judgemental attitudes. True, that partly reflects an era in the Church long since past, but that is perhaps less so than we might imagine. We can still all too easily preach forgiveness yet practise condemnation.

Paul reminds us that none of us is perfect, not even the most exalted among us – no one has the right to sit in judgement on another, for we all fall short. Yet he reminds us also that God loves us as we are, his mercy freely given and never withdrawn. It was this knowledge that shaped Paul's life and dictated all his dealings. Let it shape ours in turn.

Summary

- Turning over a new leaf isn't easy. The spirit may be willing but the flesh is weak.

- Paul was as conscious as anyone of his failure to follow Christ faithfully. Even though he had zealously followed the Jewish law, he knew he could never hope to overcome his inherent weaknesses through his own efforts.

- Frustration at our repeated disobedience can drive us to despair, leading us to feel that God may lose patience with us.

- The message of the gospel, however, is that God's nature is always to have mercy. Through Christ, he is always ready to forgive.

- We need to beware of stressing works at the cost of faith, imagining that we need to earn salvation. Our efforts to serve Christ better should be in response to his love rather than an attempt to earn or deserve it.

- Beware of being too hard on yourself, and of consequently limiting the extent of God's grace.

- Beware of being too hard on others, and of giving a false picture of the gospel and the Church.

- Let God's mercy be the decisive influence in your life.

Discussion

- Do you agree that we can be our own worst critic? Why do you think this is?

- There is always a tension between faith and works. How do you reconcile this?

- Do you think that people associate the Church today with self-righteousness or judgemental attitudes? If so, why do you think this is? Is such a view justified?

Prayer

Merciful God,
    unlike us you don't dwell on our failures.
Instead, you have invited us to acknowledge them openly before you,
    to receive your pardon
    and then to move on.
Help us to do just that –
    to accept your offer for what it is
    and then, rather than wallow in our guilt,
    to rejoice in your mercy.
Help us not simply to talk about new life
    but to live it joyfully,
    receiving each moment as your gracious gift.
Through Jesus Christ our Lord.
Amen.

Meditation of Paul

Have you ever tried turning over a new leaf?
I have,
    again,
    and again,
    and again.
Every morning I wake up and say, 'Today is going to be different!'
And every night I lie down with the knowledge that it wasn't.
For all my good intentions, I make the same mistakes
    I've always made,
    display the same old weaknesses,
    succumb to the same old temptations –
    a constant cycle of failure.
Why does it happen?
I just can't work it out,
    for I want so much to be faithful,
    more than anything else in the world,

yet somehow, before I know it, I find I've fallen again,
    unable to do even my own will, let alone God's.
It's as though there are two selves at war within me,
    one intent on good and the other on evil,
    and you don't need me to tell you which one emerges the victor.
Can it ever change?
I'd like to think so,
    but I honestly don't think it will,
    for though the spirit is willing, the flesh is weak,
    rushing, like a moth before a candle, towards its own destruction.
Do you wonder that I despair sometimes?
It's impossible not to.
Yet I shouldn't lose heart,
    because despite it all God still loves me,
    not for what one day I might be,
    but for what I am now,
    with all my sin sticking to me.
That's why he sent his Son into the world –
    not to save the righteous,
    but to rescue people like you and me,
    weak, foolish, faithless,
    unable to help ourselves.
It doesn't mean I'll stop trying;
    I'll never do that until my dying day.
But it *does* mean, however many times I fail,
    however often he finds me lying in the gutter,
    he'll be there to pick me up and set me on my way again,
    cleansed, restored, forgiven,
    the slate wiped clean, ready to start afresh,
    through his grace, a new creation!

Further reading: Romans 8:1-4

So, then, there is no longer any condemnation for those who are in
Christ Jesus, for the law of the Spirit of life in Jesus Christ has

redeemed you from the law of sin and death. For God has achieved what the law, undermined by the flesh, was incapable of doing. By sending his own Son in fallible human flesh to tackle sin, he condemned sin in the flesh, so that the underlying principles of the law might find fulfilment in those of us who walk not according to the flesh but according to the Spirit.

Suggestions for action

- Thumb through a concordance, and reflect on the passages of Scripture which speak of God's grace, mercy and forgiveness.
- If there are areas in your life where you are being too hard on yourself, let go and recognise that God has forgiven you.
- Stop being intolerant or critical of others, and strive to show the same forgiving attitude that God has shown to you.

Closing prayer

Merciful Lord,
   with hearts at peace we return to the journey of life,
   the past put behind us,
   the future full of promise.
Receive our praise,
   in the name of Christ.
Amen.

Third week

Pressing on

Opening prayer

May I do all the good I can,
    by all the means I can,
    in all the ways I can,
    in all the places I can,
    as long as I ever can,
    for Christ's sake.
Amen.

Based on the Rule of John Wesley

Introduction

Recently, I challenged a friend to a game of squash. It seemed a good idea at the time – that is, until I started to play! Two truths then swiftly dawned on me. The first was that my opponent was in a different league to me – hardly surprising, given that he played the game two or three times a week. The second was that I was a lot less fit than I thought. That, too, should have come as no surprise, for it was my first game of squash for 25 years and virtually my first serious exercise in all that time. In common with most people, however, I fondly imagined that I was still as youthful and energetic as I'd been in my teens. To realise how out of condition I'd become came as something of a shock and brought home to me the need for some kind of fitness programme to make up for the long hours stuck behind a desk.

There are clear parallels in all this with Christian discipleship. Most of us like to imagine that we are in tiptop spiritual condition, fit and eager to start out on the next leg of Christian discipleship.

The reality is somewhat different. Unconsciously, we tend to settle into a comfortable routine, rarely stretching the muscles of faith, let alone getting ourselves into the sort of shape needed to take part in a marathon and see it through to the end. Though we'd never admit it, our faith becomes an occasional pursuit rather than an ongoing commitment. We jog along casually as the mood takes us, stopping occasionally to rest and even sometimes turning back over the same old ground. It may be that we will finally complete the course, but it may equally be that we run out of steam along the way, or think we have reached the finishing line only to find ourselves disqualified at the last. Whatever else, the taking part will be a painful struggle rather than the demanding but rewarding challenge God intended. Don't deceive yourself. Don't put your trust in the efforts or achievements of yesterday. The prize is there to be grasped – are you ready to make it yours?

Activity

A spot of exercise (see page 68).

Reading: 1 Corinthians 9:24-27

Do you not know that those running in a race all take part, but only one receives the prize. Run, therefore, so that you may be the one who obtains it. Athletes wrestle to discipline their bodies, so that they may receive an award that ultimately perishes, but we strive for an imperishable award. In consequence, I do not run aimlessly, nor do I box as though I am pummelling thin air, but I subject my body to punishment to make sure that, having announced the race to others, I am not disqualified from it myself.

Comment

What is it that makes some people excel in their chosen sphere? How is it that a few individuals reach the top whilst most of us have to settle simply for being ordinary? The answer, I would suggest, lies in three simple ingredients: talent, training and practice. Unless you are naturally gifted, not even all the training and practice in the world will turn you into a champion or expert in your field. You may improve, but you will never reach the heights. To be exceptional in any sphere, sporting or otherwise, needs more than simply our own efforts. It requires God-given talent; we either have it or we don't. Yet, having said that, training and practice are vital. Even the greatest champions still make time to work with their coach. They are always seeking to improve their game, refine their technique and hone their ability. However good they are, they will never reach a point where everything is perfect and they can progress no further; there is always room for improvement. Behind apparently effortless success lie years of practice, day in, day out, until the required skill has become second nature.

Few of us will have any designs on sporting prowess, or any other, but the example of the dedicated athlete has much to teach us, as the Apostle Paul was well aware. Having travelled widely in the ancient world, and spent time in Athens and Rome, he had no doubt seen many examples of sporting competition, and what he saw there spoke powerfully of what he considered to be the essential ingredients of successful Christian discipleship. 'Do you not know', he observed, 'that though all may run in a race, only one receives the prize? Run, therefore, so that you may be the one who obtains it' (1 Corinthians 9:24).

What, then, did Paul have in mind? I think first he was drawing a parallel between an athlete's self-discipline and the part we must play in ensuring we promote our spiritual health. Discipleship is not something that takes care of itself. We cannot simply sign up and then leave the rest to God. Do that and, at best, we will stand still or, worse, we will end up going backwards rather than forwards. Faith involves dedication and commitment, the single-minded resolve and determination of an athlete in training. We need that sort of enthusiasm and self-discipline if we are to reach our potential: a determination to reach forward to new goals and to scale fresh heights each day. Each one of us needs to *work out* and *work at* our faith! If God has given us the raw materials, it is up to us to make the most of them, to make use of every resource at our disposal in order to run the race in such a way as to gain the prize. As Paul put it, in the first of his letters to the Corinthians (9:25): 'Athletes wrestle to discipline their bodies, so that they may receive an award that ultimately perishes, but we strive for an imperishable award.'

What are those resources? We know them well enough. Time for prayer and reflection, studying the Scriptures and sharing fellowship with other Christians: time to learn *of* Christ and *from* him; time to benefit from the experience of those who run alongside us. Without such things, we cannot hope to progress as we should, for our reserves will always be limited and our resources stretched. If we are serious about discipleship, we need a hunger to learn more, an eagerness to grow as Christians, and an unshakable resolve to strengthen and perfect our relationship with Christ.

That is what characterised the discipleship of Paul. He recognised that however far he had come there was further to go, that however much he understood there was more to understand. There was never any sense of having arrived; rather, a pressing on towards his ultimate goal. 'Not that I have already achieved this or reached such a goal,' he wrote to the Philippians (3:12), 'but I strive continually to make it my own, just as Christ Jesus has made me his own.'

Do we still have that same sense of purpose? Do we still have a similar yearning to grow? Or have we fallen into the trap of feeling that we have progressed as far as we need to go? The truth is this: whether we have been a Christian a day, a month, a year or a lifetime, there is still more to learn and more to understand.

If that, though, is the training, we need also to put our faith into practice, to apply it in the amphitheatre of everyday life rather than leave it somewhere on the periphery. Unless faith shows itself in action, it is useless. All the discipline and dedication that has gone before is not an end in itself, but is intended to equip us for the moment of truth. We are not called to hone our spiritual physique like some narcissistic bodybuilder, getting ourselves into trim solely for our own benefit. Instead, we must be salt and light in the world, witnesses to the love of Christ through word and deed. No, we will not always succeed, and, yes, there will always be room for improvement, but we must continue to strive each day, seeking to grow in grace and to follow more faithfully.

How does that make you feel: uncertain, overwhelmed, in despair? It could do, and it would do if that were the whole story, but of course it isn't. The last thing that Paul was saying is that the onus rests entirely on us; that somehow we must run the race relying solely on our own reserves. As we have already seen, he knew from personal experience that this was impossible; that no matter how hard we try or how much effort we put in, we cannot succeed in our own strength or through our own merit. On the contrary, our ability to run the race, and indeed to participate in it at all, is a God-given thing, made possible by his grace. He is the one who gives faith, not us; he the one who nourishes and nurtures it, who equips us to complete the course, and who accompanies us along the way. Without him all the effort and striving in the world would get us nowhere.

Where, then, are you? Are you still on track or have you started to falter? Are you moving forward or slipping back? Are you pressing on towards the goal, or running aimlessly, unsure of where you're going? God has called us to run the race, not alone but in his power. He will do his part; will we do ours?

Summary

- Three essentials underlie the success of any athlete: talent, training and practice.
- There is a sense in which these ingredients are equally important in Christian discipleship.
- We must work at our faith, ensuring that it is always growing rather than standing still.

- We need to put our faith into practice, applying it to daily life.
- We are not dependent solely on our own resources. God has put new life within us, and is constantly by our side to guide, encourage and inspire.

Discussion

- Do you regard faith as a lifetime commitment or as a casual hobby, something you dip into as the fancy takes you? Does your life back up your answer?
- In what ways can you work at your faith? What have you found most helpful in nurturing and developing it?
- In what ways does your faith show itself in practice? What difference does it make to your daily life?

Prayer

Living God,
    I talk of commitment,
    yet so often I am casual about my faith
    and complacent in discipleship.
I push you to the back of my mind,
    my thoughts preoccupied with other concerns.
I neglect your word
    and fail to make time for prayer or quiet reflection,
    thus giving myself little opportunity to hear your word.
Instead of seeking to grow in faith,
    I assume I have advanced as far as I need to.
Forgive me my feeble vision and lack of dedication.
Instil in me a new sense of purpose and a greater resolve to fulfil it,
    and so help me to achieve the prize
    to which you have called me in Jesus Christ,
    for his name's sake.
Amen.

Meditation of Paul

It's incredible,
    quite astonishing!
To think that I, Paul,
    the man who hated Jesus and everything about him,
    should have come to love him so much.
I can still scarcely credit it.
When I look back and remember the man I used to be,
    so certain of my own righteousness,
    so determined to destroy his name,
    I wonder how I ever changed.
But I did,
    totally,
    not just in incidental details,
    not simply in outward allegiance,
    but in my heart and soul,
    right down to the very core of my being.
It's as though I'm a new person,
    created afresh in the image of my Saviour,
    my every thought and impulse different than it used to be.
Not that I'm perfect, don't think I'm claiming that;
    I make my mistakes, all too often,
    sometimes despairing of ever being the person
    I would truly like to be.
Yet even then, at my lowest ebb,
    when I fail and fail again,
    I know he is with me,
    making me whole once more.
I'd have laughed at that once,
    greeted the idea with scorn
    and poured out more of my poison.
But then I met him,
    there on the Damascus Road,
    and my life was turned upside down.
He called me to be an Apostle,

an ambassador in his service,
and though I count myself the least of those who bear that name,
it is my greatest joy
and highest honour.
Not that it's been plain-sailing, mind you –
I bear my scars
and wear these chains.
And though, thanks to him, I've done a lot,
more than I could have imagined possible –
building up his Church,
advancing his kingdom –
I know deep down I've barely started,
still so many yet to reach.
So I press on with one goal in mind –
to serve him more fully,
love him more truly,
and know him more wholly,
until the day finally comes
when I shall see him and know him completely,
face to face,
one to one.

Further reading: Philippians 3:10-14

I want to know Christ and the power of his resurrection and what it means to participate in his sufferings through identifying with him in his death, if, through that, I may somehow attain to the resurrection from the dead. Not that I have already achieved this or reached such a goal, but I strive continually to make it my own, just as Christ Jesus has made me his own. Friends, I do not claim to have yet secured this for myself; but what I do is this: forgetting what is past and straining forward to what is yet in store, I give my all to reach the goal of the prize of God's heavenly call in Christ Jesus.

Suggestions for action

If you do not follow some kind of Bible-reading programme, start using one this week, and stick to it. Does your church or denomination offer a Christian training/discipleship programme? Sign up to it. Commit yourself to a Bible study or house-group series. Ensure that you make proper time this week for prayer and reflection.

Closing prayer

Lord Jesus Christ,
    give me a vision of your kingdom
    and the part you would have me play in bringing it closer,
    and so help me to strive each day towards that goal,
    for your name's sake.
Amen.

Fourth week

The one thing needed

Opening prayer

Almighty God,
> you have taught us through your Son
> that love is the fulfilling of the law.
Grant that we may love you with our whole heart
> and our neighbours as ourselves
> through Jesus Christ our Lord.
Amen.

Daily Office Revised

Introduction

The other day, while searching for some information, I came across a CD-ROM encyclopaedia that I hadn't used for years. It was a few years out of date, admittedly, but I felt sure it would contain the information I needed, so I eagerly loaded it on to my computer, believing that my search would soon be over. Then . . . disaster: I needed the registration code in order to open it, and that had long since been lost. The information I required had all been successfully installed on to my computer – in fact, there was more knowledge stored there than I could possibly know what to do with – but it was of no value whatsoever, for I lacked the one thing needed to access it. We might compare this to a car without an ignition key, an electrical appliance without a fuse, or a cash dispenser without a PIN – each promises much but yields nothing without that small but essential 'ingredient'. So it is also when it comes to faith, as the Apostle Paul reminds us in his memorable words to the Corinthians. Without love, he tells us, all else is useless. We may have all the knowledge in the world, untold gifts, unrivalled courage and unsurpassed faith, but, without love, it all counts for nothing. Few passages of Scripture are better known, few better loved, but how many of us ever stop to reflect on what Paul is saying and why he said it? We make time in this session to consider the man and his ministry, in order more fully to understand his message.

Activity
Quiz (see page 68).

Reading: 1 Corinthians 13:1-13

If I speak in the tongues of people or angels, but do not have love, I become nothing more than a deafening gong or a clashing cymbal. If I have the gift of prophecy, so that I can understand all mysteries and all knowledge, and if I have faith that can move mountains, yet do not have love, then I am nothing. If I dispense all my goods and surrender my body to be burned, yet do not have love, it profits me nothing. Love is patient and kind; it is not jealous or puffed up with its own importance, vaunting itself before others, nor does it knowingly cause offence. It does not seek its own well-being, is not easily provoked, and does not think evil or rejoice in wrongdoing but rejoices rather in the truth. It stays true, trusts, hopes and perseveres in all things.

Love is never exhausted. As for prophecies, they will end; as for tongues, they will finish; as for knowledge, it will ultimately cease. What we know and prophesy is only partial; but when the full picture is revealed, the partial will be no more. When I was a child, I thought and reasoned like a child; when I reached adulthood, I put a stop to childish ways. For the moment we see but a riddle in a mirror, then we shall see face to face; now I see only in part, but then I will fully know just as I am fully known.

These three things, then, continue: faith, hope and love; the greatest among them being love.

Comment

For many people, the very mention of Paul's name is enough to make them stop their ears and close their minds. He is seen as synonymous with complicated doctrinal arguments, obscure expositions of Scripture and an often-arid legalism. Such reservations are understandable, for much in Paul's writings is indeed confusing and can seem highly intimidating to the modern reader. Yet, on the other hand, it is to Paul that we owe some of the most memorable passages of Scripture, including those we have looked at already in this course. At the pinnacle must surely stand his celebrated chapter on love in 1 Corinthians 13, few words more beautiful, evocative and uncomplicated than these. Here, at once, is eloquent poetry and profound theology; a fusion of the sublime and the simple in words that simultaneously inspire and challenge us. Having read them at numerous wedding services, I have seen the impact they have on people, even the most atheistic of individuals spellbound by their message.

So what is it that gives his words their unique power? In part, it is the poetic aspect of Paul's language, but it is more than that. What speaks to people most of all, I believe, is the fact that his message rings true; it strikes a chord deep down in the human psyche, giving a glimpse of the way we believe life should be, and the way we believe it could be if only we were able to live by the tenets Paul speaks of. Yet that, in a sense, is simply to restate the question, for how was it that Paul could take wings and reach such heights when so much else in his writings somehow leaves us cold? After all, he was no philosopher, poet or master of rhetoric, and, as far as we know, he had no wife or family, nor any romantic attachments in his earlier life – at least, none we are told of. Yet there was, of course, one great love in his life, and that was the love of God he experienced in Christ. Legalistic he may sometimes seem but, for Paul, faith was anything but a dull, dry matter of the intellect. It revolved, rather, around an ongoing and intimate relationship: a daily experience of Christ's presence, the constant companionship of the Holy Spirit, and an ever-growing realisation of the inexhaustible love and grace of God.

For me, it is here that we must look if we are to understand the qualities of love about which Paul wrote so passionately to the Corinthians: the love that 'stays true, trusts, hopes and perseveres in all things', or, as the NIV puts it, 'always protects, always trusts, always hopes, always perseveres'. For Paul, those weren't simply fine words but a living testimony. He considered himself the least deserving, least lovable and least promising of individuals, but God had reached out to him in love, not to punish but to welcome, not to condemn but to forgive, not to deny but to affirm, not to destroy but to bring to life! If that was wonder enough, it was made all the more so by the fact that he had known another way – religion that had previously been a matter of rules and regulations, of striving in vain to earn the approval of a God who seemed remote and unapproachable. Now, in place of duty there was joy, in place of judgement there was grace, in place of law there was love!

Little wonder, then, that Paul was so concerned to guard against faith divorced from love, but he was under no illusions, well aware how easily that split between the two could happen. He had seen 'gifts' of the Spirit in the churches he had helped to found, and witnessed how easily these could destroy, unsettle and hurt if not accompanied by love. He had seen people who knew the scriptures back to front, apparently full of wisdom and understanding, yet their knowledge leading to arrogance, division and misinterpretation. He had seen people making apparently selfless gestures when, in reality, they were simply reinforcing their own sense of righteousness. He had seen Christians hung up on issues of doctrine, taken in by the latest fashion in worship, attracted by charismatic personalities instead of by Christ himself or preoccupied by religious niceties, and he had witnessed the tragic divisions, backbiting and sniping that such things can lead to. In his words on love, Paul was not just expounding theory; he was writing from personal experience of life *with* love and life *without* it.

The lesson is as important today as ever, for we can still so easily turn Christian discipleship into a matter of outward show rather than inner reality, of religious ritual rather than life-giving love. We may have committed our lives to Christ and be active members of the Church; we may attend worship Sunday by Sunday and know the Bible from cover to cover; we may never miss a day's prayer and be involved in all kinds of Christian activities and good works – but so what? None of that, in itself, means anything. If we do not do such things for love then we might as well not do them at all, for they are as far removed from God as it is possible to be. They may meet a need within us, they may feed our sense of self-worth, they may even be sincere and well intentioned, but they will never satisfy our soul or make a difference to the world we live in. True faith begins and ends in love, and without that it is nothing.

So what of Paul himself – did he manage to live up to the standards he preached, to show the sort of love he wrote of? He had every reason not to; good cause to feel hatred for those who persecuted him, bitterness towards those who questioned his authority, anger at those who opposed his work. There's no doubt that Paul would have done all he could to overcome any such feelings, but I suspect at times they found a place, and that Paul would have been the first to admit it. As he put it to the Corinthians: 'Now we see in a mirror, dimly, but then we will see face to face. Now I know only in part; then I will know fully, even as I have been fully known' (1 Corinthians 13:12, *NRSV*). For all his insight and understanding, all his faith and wisdom, he still saw himself as a beginner, a mere child on the path to adulthood, knowing he had more to learn about Christ and further to grow in his relationship with him. If you want to know about love, he says, don't look at me; look at Christ: the one who had reached out in love when he had been thrashing around in hatred, who had believed in him even when there had seemed no grounds for doing so, who owed him nothing, yet had given all!

We are back, of course, to where we started: to the love of God in Christ. There, says Paul, is the love that bears all things, believes all things, hopes all things, endures all things. That's where we see love, in the one who was love incarnate – love such as the world has never seen before. In him is the key to everything Paul ever did, said and achieved, for though we may marvel at this remarkable man, he would have us marvel at someone more remarkable still: at the one who showed such love to him and who longs to show such love to all.

Summary

- Some of the writings of Paul can seem daunting, but his words concerning love are widely celebrated, having inspired countless people across the centuries.
- The heart of Paul's message sprang from his own experience of the love of God, which had so radically transformed his life. He knew that a faith based on law rather than love was a burden rather than a blessing.
- Paul, further, had seen the danger of religion bereft of love. Far from drawing people closer, it divided them from God and one another.
- The danger is just as real today. We can very easily lose sight of what faith is ultimately all about.
- Paul had every reason not to love, having experienced hatred and evil first-hand, yet he knew that love was finally the only way of conquering such things.
- Equally, Paul was well aware that his love was flawed, whether for God or for others. To see true love, he tells us, and to have it flow through our lives, we must look to Christ, who demonstrated it so powerfully through his life, death and resurrection.

Discussion

- Do you agree with Paul that without love all else is nothing, or do you think he is going too far? Is this the language of poetic hyperbole or profound truth?
- How would you define love? What would you see as the essentials underlying it?
- How far is love the motivating factor behind all our actions?
- How does Paul's teaching about love affect our attitude to people of other faiths, with whose beliefs we might disagree?

Prayer

Lord Jesus Christ,
  you summed up the law in one simple word: 'love'.
Forgive us that though we often talk about love,
  we rarely show it in practice.
Forgive us everything in our lives that has denied that love:
  the angry words and unkind comments,
  the thoughtless deeds and careless actions;
  the sorrow we have brought rather than joy,
  and hurt rather than healing;
  the care we have failed to express,
  support we have refused to offer
  and forgiveness we have been unwilling to extend.
Help us to look to you who showed us love in action –
  a love that stays true,
  trusts,
  hopes
  and perseveres in all things;
  and help us truly to realise that unless we have that,
  then all our words, faith and religion count for nothing.
Amen.

Meditation of Paul

He taught me the meaning of love:
    what it really means to say, 'I love you.'
Slowly,
    gently,
    he taught me –
    not through words,
    nor through gestures,
    but through showing me love in action.
I thought I'd understood,
    that I loved as much as the next man, maybe more.
Not perhaps as a husband loves his wife, or a father his children –
    there's not been time for that, sadly –
    but deeper,
    beyond such natural ties –
    my fellow apostles,
    my family in Christ,
    my fellow human beings.
And I did love in my own way – of course I did;
    my only goal,
    my single aim,
    to help them,
    serve them,
    reach them.
And yet, despite all that, I sometimes wondered
    if I'd ever loved at all,
    for deep down, in my heart of hearts,
    I knew it was all about me –
    my preaching,
    my striving,
    my loving;
    my efforts,
    my successes,
    my ambitions –
    all finally for my *own* satisfaction,

and even, I fear, my own glory as much as his.
It's human, I realise that, or so at least we tell ourselves,
    but is it,
    or, at least, does it have to be?
For when I look at Jesus –
    all he did for me –
    I see a different truth,
    a different kind of love:
    patient,
    kind,
    humble,
    not serving self or seeking gain,
    but putting others first –
    a love that knows me as I am,
    understands my faults,
    yet still believes in me;
    that, though I turn away, accepts me,
    even dies for me!
That's what it means, this thing called love,
    seeing the worst,
    believing the best,
    asking nothing,
    and giving all.
I thought I'd understood, all those years ago,
    but I hadn't, hardly at all.
I'm still learning even now,
    still struggling to let go of self.
I can't do it alone,
    I've come to realise that at last.
I need his help, his love flowing through me,
    and I'll carry on praying for that,
    striving for that,
    until my dying day,
    for I understand now that without love all else is nothing.

Further reading: Romans 13:8-10

Owe no one anything, except to love one another; for the one who loves another has fulfilled the law. The commandments, 'You shall not commit adultery; You shall not murder; You shall not steal; You shall not covet'; and any other commandment, are summed up in this word, 'Love your neighbour as yourself.' Love does no wrong to a neighbour; therefore love is the fulfilling of the law. (*NRSV*)

Suggestions for action

Reflect on your worship, your relationships, your attitudes and your faith, and ask how far they are motivated by love and how far by duty. Open your life afresh to the love of God, and ask that it may flow through you to others.

Closing prayer

Gracious God,
    take the little love we have.
Nurture, deepen and expand it,
    until we have learned what love really means,
    until your love flows through our hearts,
    until love is all in all.
Through Jesus Christ our Lord.
Amen.

Fifth week

_____ _True contentment_ _____

Opening prayer

Lord, whose way is perfect,
  help me always to trust in your goodness,
  that walking with you
  and following you in all simplicity,
  I may possess a quiet and contented mind
  and may cast all care on you,
  for you care for me.
Amen.

Christina Rossetti

Introduction

The theme of contentment reminds me of that wonderful old fable told by Aesop concerning a dog that came across a piece of meat. Trotting happily home with its unexpected prize, it came to a bridge over a river, from which it spotted its reflection in the water below. Assuming this was another dog with a piece of meat similar to its own, the foolish creature opened its mouth to grab it, intent on making off with both pieces. The result, of course, was that it ended up with nothing, the morsel it dropped swept away on the current. We smile at that story, don't we, knowing the eventual outcome even before it happens and recognising the absurdity of the dog's actions. Do we though, I wonder, recognise similar absurdity in ourselves? As ever, Aesop put his finger here on a fundamental flaw in human nature: our never-ending desire for more. So often, just like that dog, we fail to savour what we have as we dwell on the things we haven't. If that is folly purely in human terms, it is all the more so in the context of Christian faith, for our hope and happiness are ultimately rooted in something far deeper than immediate material satisfaction. Today we focus on two passages of Paul on the subject of contentment; passages that afford us a valuable lesson in counting our blessings now, and remembering those blessings yet to come.

Activity

Building blocks (see page 69).

Readings
Philippians 4:4-7, 10-12

Rejoice in the Lord always; I repeat, rejoice! Let your serenity of mind be plain to all. The Lord is near, so do not brood over anything, but in every circumstance acquaint God with your needs through thankful prayers of supplication, and the peace of God that exceeds all human comprehension will encircle your hearts and minds in Christ Jesus. I exult greatly in the Lord that, after all this time, your concern for me has been rekindled; indeed, I realise now that you were concerned all along, but were denied the opportunity to show it. Not that I considered myself to be in need, for I have learned to be content whatever the circumstances I am facing. I know what it is to be brought low, and what it is to have my cup overflowing. In all situations, I have learned the secret of being well filled and of going hungry, of having much and having little.

1 Timothy 6:6-8

There is great gain in godliness combined with contentment; for just as we brought nothing into the world it is certain that we can take nothing out of it. So, then, if we have food and clothing, we will be satisfied with these.

49

Comment

'Happiness,' we were once told, 'is a cigar called Hamlet.' We all knew, of course, that this wasn't true, but therein lay the strength of the advertisement in question. It skilfully played on the foolishness of the claim, bringing a smile to our lips and so subconsciously endearing us to the product. There is a sense in which all advertisements convey a similar message. Their sole purpose is to convince us that our happiness will be increased if we buy the item in question, whether it is a new car, a dishwasher, a packet of cigarettes or a holiday abroad. Each is subtly portrayed as the one little extra we really need to have, and though intellectually we may know the claims are baseless, subliminally we find it hard to resist the siren voices.

So where do we find contentment? According to Paul, the answer is very simple: 'if we have food and clothing, we will be satisfied with these'. Is that true of us? In what way does it or should it apply to daily life? It is easy to be precious about this, and to shake our heads over the evils of materialism, suggesting that possessions are the root of all our ills. No doubt, there is truth in such a claim yet we all enjoy our modern-day standard of living, I as much as anyone. Which of us, if pushed, would willingly sacrifice our car, television, hi-fi, washing machine, computer and so forth? Deep down, we may know that these do not guarantee happiness, and we may even have a sneaking suspicion that we pay a hidden price for them in terms of our spiritual health and inner well-being, yet should anyone threaten to take them away we would very quickly change our tune.

Possessions in themselves are not wrong, so much as a hankering after them at the cost of all else, and it is here, I think, that we glimpse the malaise of our time. We are part of a world in which we both want and expect more, and this expectation is constantly fed by a combination of advertising and peer pressure. Which parent hasn't felt that they must buy their child the latest fashion or toy if they are not to feel the odd one out? Which adult hasn't spotted a car, a house or a garden and wished it could be theirs?

Which of us hasn't yearned for better pay, a better home, better prospects? To a point, it's natural and healthy that we should, so long as our desire for such things doesn't prevent us from appreciating what we already have. Yet isn't that what so often happens? We see the latest hi-tech gadget in the shop window and we must have it. We catch a glimpse of someone else's lifestyle and, all of a sudden, we feel unhappy with our lot. If only we had that, we tell ourselves, then we would be content, able to sit back and enjoy life, but if we do finally splash out and satisfy our whim, something else always seems to catch the eye instead.

What a contrast between all this and those words of the Apostle Paul to the Philippians: 'I have learned to be content whatever the circumstances' (4:11). An astonishing claim that becomes still more astounding when we pause for a moment to consider the situation in which he wrote and the experiences he had faced. He didn't write from a situation of comfort or security, nor as someone who had made his way in the world and who now enjoyed a relaxed and untroubled existence. On the contrary, he wrote from prison, incarcerated for his faith, having endured suffering and deprivations such as most of us can scarcely imagine. 'As servants of God,' he writes, 'we have commended ourselves in every way, through great endurance, in afflictions, hardships, calamities, beatings, imprisonments, riots, labours, sleepless nights, hunger. We are treated as impostors, and yet are true; as unknown, and yet are well known; as dying, but see – we are alive; as punished, and yet not killed; as sorrowful, yet always rejoicing; as poor, yet making many rich; as having nothing, and yet possessing everything' (2 Corinthians 6:4-5, 8b-10, *NRSV*).

Life had been no bed of roses for Paul, quite the opposite, and yet he could talk about being content, of 'possessing everything'! Despite the fact that, in human terms, he had every reason to be unhappy with his lot; despite the constant setbacks he had faced, the pain and humiliation he endured, the thorn in flesh he so long wrestled with; he had learned to be truly satisfied. In Christ, he believed, he had discovered true purpose in life, the one thing that really matters and that puts all else into perspective; a joy, peace and fulfilment that nothing, not even death itself, could take away.

As the book of Proverbs puts it, 'The fear of the Lord leads to life: Then one rests content, untouched by trouble' (Proverbs 19:23, *NIV*). Or as Paul wrote earlier in that same letter to the Corinthians (4:16-17), 'We are not discouraged, for even though we seem outwardly debilitated, inwardly we are being renewed every day. For the inconsequential affliction we currently face is preparing for us an eternal weight of glory beyond measure.'

So, what of us: have we learned to be content in all circumstances? More to the point, have we learned to be content in *any* circumstances? Or are we always trying to fit that last bit extra on to our plate? The testimony of Paul, on one level, counsels us simply to be happy with what we have; to stop and count our blessings, recognising all the good things that God has given. It calls us to let go of our hankering for more and to appreciate all we have received in so many ways already. That, in itself, would be a sufficient lesson to take away, but what Paul has to say goes much further. In the daily experience of God's love, he tells us, lies true fulfilment, an inner quietness such as this world cannot give. We may not be rich in human terms, but we all have access to far greater riches: a tranquillity of mind and spirit besides which all else pales into insignificance; a confidence in God's eternal purpose that can never be shaken; an inner assurance that nothing will ever destroy. No wonder Paul had learned to be content!

Summary

- We live in a world that measures contentment in terms of material possessions. These have a very real place in our lives, but they are not everything.
- Paul spoke of being completely content, even though his experiences in life might lead us to expect the opposite.
- The secret of Paul's contentment was his faith, and his unshakable conviction that nothing in life or death could separate him from the love of God in Christ.
- We can apply Paul's words at the level of sound common sense.

Until we learn to stop seeking more, we will never appreciate what we have.

- For the Christian, his words speak more deeply of the hope and new life we share in Christ. We too rest secure in a loving purpose that goes beyond this world.

Discussion

- How far do we seek contentment in possessions? How far do these actually make us content? Have there been times when they have brought the opposite?
- What do you value most in your life? Where does God rank in your list of priorities? Does the way you live lend support to your answer?
- How far do you think it is possible to be content in even the most adverse of circumstances? In what way might this be true?
- What circumstances ought we never to be content with?

Prayer

Loving God,
    help us to recognise that though serving Christ
    may involve sacrifice and self-denial,
    it also brings lasting fulfilment
    and an inner contentment such as this world can never bring.
Teach us that you are able to satisfy our deepest needs,
    our spiritual hunger and thirst,
    granting us a peace that nothing will be able to shake,
    however fierce the storms of life may be.
Open our eyes to the true riches that you alone can offer,
    the blessings that you hold in store for all your people.
In your name, we ask it.
Amen.

Meditation of Paul

Was I happy with my lot?
Well, as a matter of fact, I wasn't,
   not at first, anyway.
Oh, I gave thanks, don't get me wrong –
   I marvelled each day at the love of Christ
   and rejoiced constantly at the awesome grace
   he'd shown to me,
   but for all that there was much I found difficult,
   far more than I'd ever bargained on.
It wasn't the weariness,
   the endless travel,
   the days, weeks, even months without a rest –
   I could cope with those, despite my infirmities.
But when the hostility began,
   the beatings,
   the stone-throwing,
   the interminable hours rotting in a prison cell,
   that's when it became hard to bear,
   when I began to wonder just what I'd got myself into.
You wouldn't believe the things I endured –
   the hunger,
   the pain,
   the privations –
   enough to break anyone,
   crush the strongest of spirits.
And yet, somehow, they weren't able to do that,
   for in my darkest moments
   I always found the strength I needed –
   a word of encouragement,
   a sign of hope,
   a light dawning –
   and I came to realise that Christ was with me even there,
   especially there,
   in my time of need.

I may have been hungry,
    but I had food in plenty for my soul.
I may have been broken in body,
    but my spirit had been made whole.
I may have been poor in the things of this world,
    but I was rich in the things of God.
It didn't take away the pain, I can't claim that –
    the hardship, the fear and the suffering were just as real,
    just as terrible –
    but it changed the way I saw them,
    my perspective on life, on death,
    on everything, was transformed for ever.
I had joy in my heart,
    peace which passed all understanding,
    and the promise of treasure in heaven –
    whatever else might be taken from me,
    nothing could take away those.
It was enough, and more than enough!
I had learned to be content.

Further reading: 2 Corinthians 1:8-11

We do not want you to be unaware, brothers and sisters, of the affliction we experienced in Asia; for we were so utterly, unbearably crushed that we despaired of life itself. Indeed, we felt that we had received the sentence of death so that we would not rely on ourselves but on God who raises the dead. He who rescued us from so deadly a peril will continue to rescue us; on him we have set our hope that he will rescue us again, as you also join in helping us by your prayers, so that many will give thanks on our behalf for the blessing granted us through the prayers of many.

Suggestions for action

- Give thanks for all you have received. Make time to recognise all the things for which you have reason to be grateful. Stop and enjoy them while you can.
- Instead of buying something extra, why not, for a change, give something up!
- Remember that God is with you, whatever your circumstances, his love in Christ unfailing. Live each day from that perspective.

Closing prayer

Gracious God,
  teach me to celebrate the innumerable blessings
  you shower upon me each day,
  but teach me also to recognise that this world
  offers only a foretaste of the riches you hold in store.
Teach me to celebrate all I have received,
  but to set my heart first on your kingdom
  and to show my gratitude for all your many gifts
  by offering back my life in your service,
  to the glory of your name.
Amen.

Sixth week

So much more to say

Opening prayer

God,
   be in my head,
   and in my understanding;
   God be in mine eyes,
   and in my looking;
   God be in my mouth,
   and in my speaking;
   God be in my heart,
   and in my thinking;
   God be at mine end,
   and at my departing.
Amen.

Sarum Primer

Introduction

Some people simply don't know when to stop, do they? We've all met them, I'm quite sure – infuriating individuals who somehow seem able to talk *ad infinitum* without ever once pausing to draw breath. We wait for the chance to jump in, either to excuse ourselves or to have our say, but somehow the opportunity never comes. On the other hand, there are those who don't know when to start – those who are so painfully shy that it's almost an ordeal to spend time with them. Try though we might to initiate a conversation, the most we can hope for is a one-sentence or even one-word reply. The ideal, of course, is somewhere in between, and thankfully that's where most of us, in social exchanges at least, are to be found. But how about when it comes to sharing our faith? Most of us here, I suspect, fall into the tongue-tied category, anything more than the briefest of interjections something of a rarity. In our reading today, we see the former category, as the Apostle Paul experiences an off-day of monumental proportions and suffers the sort of humiliation that is the dread of every public speaker. His example is not one to emulate, but it is worth reflecting on nonetheless, for it asks a simple but important question. Put on trial for our faith, of which would we rather be accused: having said too much in our zeal for the cause of Christ, or, on the contrary, having said nothing at all?

Activity

Potted history (see page 70).

Reading: Acts 20:7-11

On the first evening of the Sabbath, the disciples having assembled to break bread, Paul preached to them and, conscious that he was due to depart the next day, he talked on past midnight. Now there were a number of oil-lamps in the upstairs room where they had gathered, and as Paul continued still longer with his sermon, a young man called Eutychus, who was perched on a window sill, sank into a torpor and fell from the third storey, and was assumed to be dead. Paul rushed down and cradled him in his arms, saying, 'Don't be alarmed. He's still alive!' And he went back upstairs, broke bread, and, having eaten this, once more talked at length until dawn broke, after which he finally departed.

Comment

When did you last hear a really boring sermon, a sermon so tedious that you found yourself shuffling in your seat, looking at your watch, exploring the permutations of the hymn numbers, and generally wondering how much longer the preacher could possibly go on? If that rings bells for you, then you will easily be able to empathise with the young man in the passage above. I can never read the story without feeling amazed that it has found its way into Scripture, for I'm quite sure that it represents an incident that Paul would have preferred to forget. Here he was, the great missionary and ambassador of the early Church, a man usually able to communicate the gospel in a most wonderful way, suffering an experience that would be enough to put most people off ever preaching again. Not only does a member of the congregation start to doze – that, in itself, is humiliating enough – but the unfortunate young man contrives in his torpor to fall from an upstairs window and crash to the ground below, dropping off, you might say, in more ways than one! Why? Quite simply because, as the NIV so bluntly puts it, 'Paul talked on and on'. True, there were extenuating circumstances – as Luke takes pains to tell us, there were many lamps burning, the implication being that perhaps fumes rather than boredom were to blame for the young man's unexpected siesta. Read on, though, and this looks increasingly like clutching at straws, for what does Paul do when he discovers that the unfortunate fellow has escaped serious harm? He carries on where he left off, and continues through the night until dawn!

So how was it that Paul, an experienced speaker, could make such a mistake? How could he be so apparently thick-skinned? The answer, I think, is given in the first verse of the passage: 'On the evening of the Sabbath, the disciples having assembled to break bread, Paul preached to them and, conscious that he was due to depart the next day, he talked on past midnight' (Acts 20:7). Here was the problem: Paul planned to move on the next day, so this was his last chance to speak and he wanted to make the most of his opportunity. He still had so much more to say, so much he wanted to tell them. There was his dramatic conversion on the Damascus Road for a start – that alone could have kept him going for a sermon series. Add to that his experiences preaching the gospel, the places he'd visited and the responses he'd received, the

59

people he'd met and those he'd worked with, the challenges he'd faced and situations he'd come up against, and you can begin to understand, if not applaud, his over-enthusiasm. It wasn't so much that *he* had more to say as that he believed *God* had more to say as well.

On the one hand, of course, he should have known better, for he had stressed often enough that no one can begin to express the wonder of God however hard they try; that whatever we may say about him, whatever we may learn or experience, there is always more to be revealed. Had he preached all the next day, the next week or even the next year, he would still not have exhausted the message of God's love or shared the full riches of the gospel! As the writer of John's Gospel so eloquently put it, 'Jesus did countless other things; so many that, were every one of them to be listed, I doubt that the world itself could contain all the books that would have to be written' (John 21:25). Did Paul not realise he was setting himself an impossible task? I've no doubt he did, but the fact was that he could scarcely contain his enthusiasm, the good news bubbling up within him so that he felt compelled to share it! He wanted to tell these people who had gathered to hear him of everything Jesus had done in his life. He wanted to encourage them in their faith, to inspire them to mission and evangelism in turn, to lead them forward in their own journey of discipleship. He wanted others to see, hear and know for themselves the reality of Christ in their hearts. The joy he had discovered in Christ burned within him with an all-consuming passion, and he could not bring himself to keep silent.

Here lies the key to understanding not simply this single incident but the whole of Paul's life and ministry, or, in other words, the man and his mission. Paul recognised more swiftly and clearly than anyone else in the early Church that the gospel was good news not simply for a few but for all, and not only for then but for always. His vision was to extend the life and witness of the Church beyond Judea to the ends of the earth; to proclaim Christ crucified and risen whenever and wherever he could find the opportunity. Here was a truly global vision – a burning conviction that just as Christ died for the whole world so the whole world needed to hear that message. This was the driving force behind his ministry – the motivation that spurred him forward despite all the rigours he faced, obstacles that confronted him and hostility he endured.

How would Paul's approach have gone down today? The answer, I suspect, is not very well. For one thing, he lived in an age of great orators, when long drawn-out speeches were the norm, whereas we live in a sound-bite era in which people are used to slick, glossy and, above all, short presentations. For another thing, in Paul's time the gospel was literally *news* in that many had never heard it before. Today, people consider it old hat, few ready to give it a second hearing. Above all, we live in a multicultural world in which there are many faiths and the potential for antipathy between them, as witnessed in the horrific destruction on the twin towers of the World Trade Center in New York, together with so many people within them. To preach Christ without considering those we preach to would serve only to alienate rather than communicate his love. To talk rather than listen, engage in a monologue rather than a dialogue, is a recipe for disaster, for it can only lead to further schism and deeper estrangement. Yet, having said all that, we nevertheless need today something of Paul's passion and enthusiasm. In an increasingly secular age, we need to give people the chance to hear again the message of the gospel. In an era when the Church is not so much despised as considered irrelevant, we need to show how faith makes a difference to everyday life, speaking of Christ in a way that is fresh, natural and relevant to our modern age. In a society where people are searching hungrily for meaning, we need to make known the loving purpose of God revealed in Christ. In a world where people are willing to slaughter senselessly in the name of faith, we need to live and make known the way of love. Sensitively, yes; at the right time and in the right way; but we need to communicate it nonetheless, and if we had even a fraction of Paul's irrepressible desire to share *his* faith, what an impact we could make.

I doubt that Paul received an invitation to visit the Church in

Troas a second time, though I can't be sure. One thing, though, is certain: had he not had that burning desire to proclaim Christ, then there would have been no invitation for him or anyone else, for the Church and the Christian faith would soon have been a thing of the past. Similarly, unless we do our bit today, there may well be no Church or Christian faith tomorrow. Are you fulfilling your role as a witness to Christ? Does your faith mean enough for you to want to share it? Or, to put it more simply, how many would hear the gospel were it down solely to you? It's a sobering thought, isn't it?

Summary

- Even Paul had his off-days. Preaching at Troas, he went on so long that a member of his congregation nodded off, with almost catastrophic consequences.
- The problem was that time was limited, and Paul wanted to communicate as much as he could concerning the gospel. Such was his enthusiasm that he could scarcely contain himself.
- This enthusiasm provides the key to understanding Paul, both in terms of the man and the mission. His overriding aim throughout his life as a Christian was to proclaim Christ, and his was a vision that knew no boundaries, always wanting to reach out yet further, in step with the all-encompassing love of God.
- Times have changed since Paul's day, and, for a variety of reasons, it is probably harder now to share the gospel. We live in a society in which many are agnostic or atheists, and in which many others represent other faiths. We need to present the gospel with sensitivity if we are not to do more harm than good. Nonetheless, the gospel needs to be heard today as much as ever.
- Without Paul, there would probably be no Church or Christian faith today. Without us playing our part, there may well be no Church or Christian faith tomorrow.

Discussion

- When did you last communicate the joy you have found in Christ?
- In what ways, if any, do you share your faith? What things hold you back from doing so?
- How would you approach sharing your faith, given the opportunity? What things would you want to focus on? What does your faith mean to you?

Prayer

Sovereign God,
    you have given us so much to share,
    more than we can ever begin to express.
You have showered us with your blessings,
    touching our lives in innumerable ways.
You have given us joy that knows no bounds,
    mercy beyond all our deserving,
    hope that can never be exhausted,
    peace that passes understanding,
    and love that exceeds anything we can ever ask or think of.
Teach us to share those gifts with others,
    to tell joyfully and spontaneously of everything
    that you have done
    and all you mean to us,
    to the glory of your name.
Amen.

Meditation of Paul

It was foolish of me –
    inexcusable really –
    yet at the time I just couldn't help myself.

I had so much to share, you see,
    so many things I wanted to tell,
    and although I knew I ought to cut it short,
    I just couldn't bring myself to do it,
    always wanting to add one thing more.
I could see they were growing restless,
    heads starting to nod and eyelids drooping –
    the signs were clear enough –
    yet, somehow, even then I carried on . . .
    and on . . .
    and on.
We'd probably still be there now, but for that poor lad Eutychus.
What a business it was!
What an embarrassment!
Not just a thump to his head
    but a blow to my esteem!
It's never happened before –
    someone dropping off like that, if you'll pardon the pun –
    and once I had time to reflect I felt a right fool,
    ashamed I could be so thick-skinned.
That was later, though,
    at the time, I was simply shocked –
    we *all* were –
    my only concern to ensure the boy was unharmed.
He was, thank the Lord,
    and I should have taken that as my cue to leave,
    but what did I do then?
You've guessed it:
    I carried on where I'd left off.
All right, that may seem strange,
    curiously insensitive,
    but, be fair, I could hardly finish the evening on that note,
    could I?
They'd come to hear of Jesus,
    and that's what I wanted to send them home with –
    the message of the gospel ringing in their ears

rather than excited chatter about young men
falling out of windows!
I'm doing it again, aren't I?
Rambling on, like before.
So I'll stop now before someone else gets hurt.
I've learned my lesson –
 well, almost! –
but I tell you this:
when it comes to Jesus,
and proclaiming the faith,
I'd rather have too much to say,
than end up saying nothing at all.
Wouldn't you?

Further reading: Romans 15:17-21

In Christ Jesus, then, I have reason to boast of my work for God.
For I will not venture to speak of anything except what Christ has
accomplished through me to win obedience from the Gentiles, by
word and deed, by the power of signs and wonders, by the power
of the Spirit of God, so that from Jerusalem and as far around as
Illyricum I have fully proclaimed the good news of Christ. Thus I
make it my ambition to proclaim the good news, not where Christ
has already been named, so that I do not build on someone else's
foundation, but as it is written, 'Those who have never been told
of him shall see, and those who have never heard of him shall
understand.' (*NRSV*)

Suggestions for action

Don't just talk of evangelism; talk of Christ!

Closing prayer

Loving Lord,
   we have so much to share –
   save us from ever keeping it to ourselves.
Amen.

Appendix 1

Activities

First week: Admitting we're wrong

Slippery spellings

Using a dictionary, or selecting from the list below, choose ten words for a spelling test. Distribute pen and paper, and tell the group that you are going to test their spelling. Slowly call out the words on your list, repeating them as necessary, and giving members of the group ample time for each. When everyone is finished, run through the correct spellings. Ask participants how many they got right and how many they got wrong. Then ask if anyone is willing to share which spellings they got wrong or are people too embarrassed to admit their mistakes. Move from this to a brief discussion of what mistakes we might find it awkward or even impossible to acknowledge.

Commonly misspelled words (You may prefer to choose your own words, so as to catch participants cold):

onomatopoeia; accommodation; diarrhoea; medieval; supersede; desiccate; embarrass; harassment; seize; millennium; vermilion; idiosyncrasies; minuscule; sacrilegious; privilege; weird; analogous; pavilion; hyperbole; psychedelic; numinous; diaphanous; extraneous; psoriasis; supercilious.

Second week: By the grace of God

Word puzzle

Distribute pens and paper, then give group members three words to write down: WRONG, RIGHT, and GRACE. Ask whether, by changing one letter at a time to make a new word, it is possible to change WRONG to RIGHT, or WRONG to GRACE (I was able to complete one of these in eight steps, but not the other). Move from this to a brief discussion on why we can do some things but not others. Ask whether people still make resolutions at such times as Lent or the New Year, and, if so, whether they are able to keep them.

Third week: Pressing on

A spot of exercise

Devise a simple series of exercises (gauged according to the age and health of group members!), and see how many members of the group are able to complete them – for example, touching one's toes; clapping hands behind one's back; clasping hands with one hand behind one's back and one over one's shoulder; sit-ups. Talk together about fitness, and discuss briefly how we might apply this to Christian discipleship.

Fourth week: The one thing needed

Quiz

History, literature and legend are full of couples celebrated for their love. Can you identify the following?

1. The love of this couple created by Emily Brontë will forever be associated with the fells of Yorkshire around Haworth.

2. A couple in Arthurian romance, who have subsequently inspired opera and poetry.

3. First mentioned in a ballad of Henry Woodfall, these names have become synonymous with the ideal elderly couple.

4. An actor and actress whose sometimes-stormy relationship seems to have drifted in and out of love.

5. A romance from antiquity, famously portrayed by the above couple.

6. An unlikely couple of complete opposites in a folk tale immortalised by Walt Disney.

7. Who inspired the love of Charlotte Brontë's Jane Eyre?

8. Their love led to a British constitutional crisis.

9. The epitome of romantic tragic love, exemplified in the play by Shakespeare and subsequent overture by Tchaikovsky.

10. A couple created by Thomas Hardy, whose relationship was blighted by misfortune and misunderstanding.

Talk together about the ingredients of a loving relationship, and discuss briefly the implications of this in terms of Christian discipleship.

Fifth week: True contentment

Building blocks

For this activity you will need a good supply of children's building bricks, or something similar. (You could, perhaps, if you want to make things really hard, use playing cards.) Challenge members of the group, stacking bricks singly, one on top of the other, to build the biggest tower possible within one minute. (Depending on the number of bricks you have, participants can take turns in pairs, or in groups of three or four at a time.) Afterwards, discuss how this exercise might relate to contentment. For example, did it teach us anything about learning when enough is enough?

Sixth week: So much more to say

Potted history

Give participants a pen and paper, and ask them to jot down three statements (maximum length: five words) that sum up their character, life history, faith, interests or profession. Discuss afterwards how easy or difficult they found it to choose what to say and what not to say. Talk through the implications of this in terms of sharing our faith with others.

Appendix 2

Answers

Second week: By the grace of God

WRONG, PRONG, PRANG, PRANK, CRANK, CRACK, TRACK, TRACE, GRACE

Fourth week: The one thing needed

1. Catherine (Earnshaw) and Heathcliff
2. Tristam and Ysolde
3. Darby and Joan
4. Elizabeth Taylor and Richard Burton
5. Antony and Cleopatra
6. Beauty and the Beast
7. Mr Rochester
8. Edward and Mrs Simpson
9. Romeo and Juliet
10. Tess (of the D'Urbevilles) and Angel (Clare)
    (or, indeed, almost any couple in Hardy's novels!)

Also in this series:
Living with questions – exploring faith and doubt
Something to share – communicating the good news
Prayer – the fundamental questions
Unsung gifts – the Spirit at work in the New Testament
Love – the key to it all
Discipleship – the journey of faith
Women of faith – what they teach us

Also by Nick Fawcett:
No ordinary man (books 1 and 2)
Resources for reflective worship on the person of Jesus

The unfolding story
Resources for reflective worship on the Old Testament

Grappling with God (books 1-4)
Old Testament studies for personal and small-group use

To put it another way
Resources for reflective worship on the Parables

Are you listening?
Honest prayers about life

Prayers for all seasons (books 1 and 2)
A comprehensive resource for public worship

Getting it across
One hundred talks for family worship

Decisions, decisions
A Lent study course

Promises, promises
An Advent study course

Daily prayer
A book of daily devotions

All the above titles are available from your local Christian bookshop
or direct from Kevin Mayhew Ltd, telephone 01449 737978,
fax: 01449 737834, email: sales@kevinmayhewltd.com